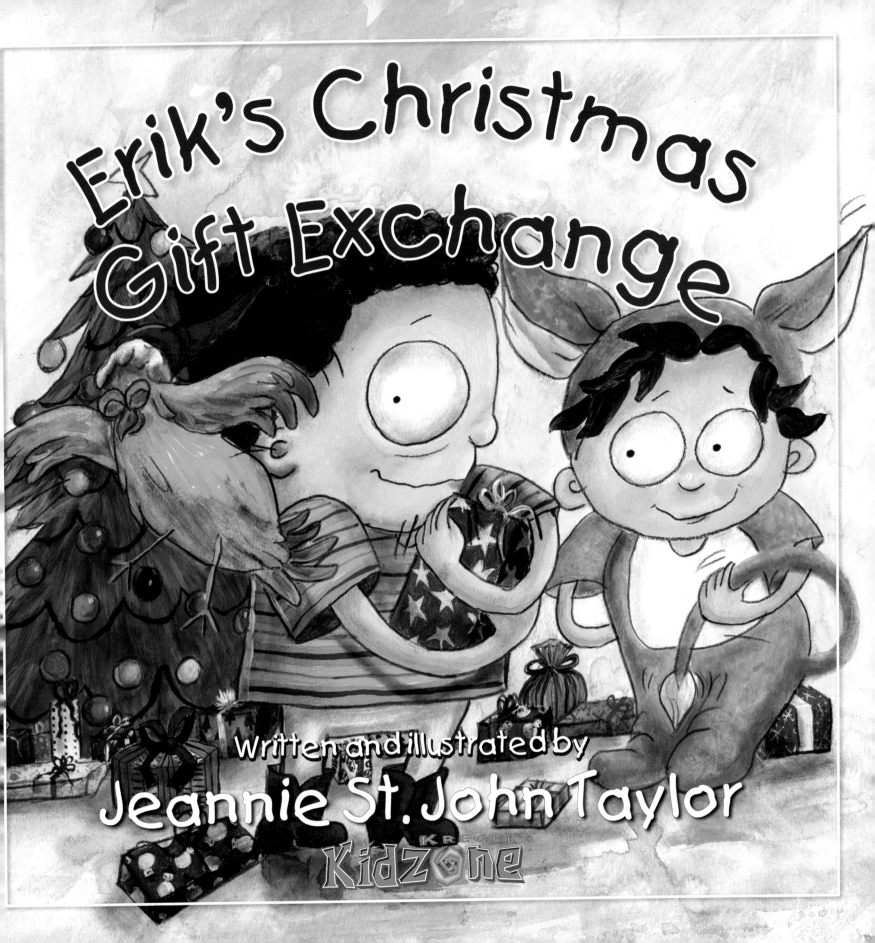

Erik's Christmas Gift Exchange

Written and illustrated by

Jeannie St. John Taylor

Kregel Kidzone

**Jeannie would love to hear from you.
She answers all e-mails personally.
She can be reached at Jeannie@kregel.com.**

Erik's Christmas Gift Exchange

© 2006 by Jeannie St. John Taylor

Published by Kregel Kidzone, an imprint of Kregel Publications, Grand Rapids, Michigan 49501.

ISBN 0-8254-3660-5

Printed in China

**To the newlyweds,
Tevin and Kirsten Taylor**

I jam my wallet into my pocket and race to grab a spot in line with Casper. It's noisy because everyone's so excited about the bus trip to the mall—to buy presents for the class Christmas gift exchange.

"Whose name did you draw?" Casper asks.

"Todd's."

Casper gawks at me like I said "Darth Vader."

But before he has a chance to say anything, and before I can say "I'm not too happy about it myself," Mrs. Burdon walks up with Chuck.

"Erik, would you and Casper like to add Chuck to your group? We have an extra boy."

"Sure!" we say.

Just after we board the bus an idea explodes across my brain. "There are three of us, and there were three Wise Men. They crossed the desert to take gifts to Baby Jesus. We're crossing town to buy gifts. So let's be Wise Men."

Sophia peeks over the top of our seat. "Can I be Mary?"

We three kings say, "sure," together.

By the time the bus pulls up to the mall, everyone has asked to be someone in the Christmas story. Everyone but Todd. I think maybe he should be King Herod, because Todd and Herod are both so mean, but I don't say it out loud.

Before we pile off the bus, Mrs. Burdon reminds us to stay in our groups for safety.

So, we three Wise Men march off together toward the toy store, Sophia-Mary strolls into a department store with Laura-the-sheep, and Riley-Joseph heads to the electronics store with Buzz-the-shepherd.

As soon as we get inside Casper buys a unicorn-shaped bottle of bubbles for Laura, so he'll have time to play the electronic games.

I *see* angels Maddy and Hannah giggling over some enormous stuffed animals, and Chuck picks out a toy dinosaur. But I can't find anything. I don't want to give Todd a gift because he always makes fun of me. I wish I had drawn someone else's name.

**Then I see it. The most awesome car ever invented.
It's bigger than my hand and shimmers like a rainbow.**

It's fast. The perfect gift . . . for *me!* I count my money. Twice. I have enough to buy the car plus one dollar and a few pennies extra. I pay for the car and yell for the other two Wise Men to follow me.

We speed to the dollar store across the mall, where I grab an apple-sized rubber ball and hurl it against the floor. Hard. It doesn't bounce very high, but that doesn't matter. Todd doesn't need a great present.

RAPPIN

PAPE

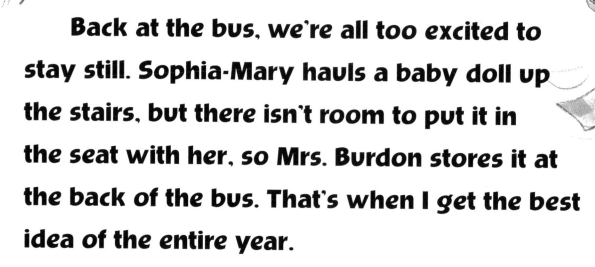

Back at the bus, we're all too excited to stay still. Sophia-Mary hauls a baby doll up the stairs, but there isn't room to put it in the seat with her, so Mrs. Burdon stores it at the back of the bus. That's when I get the best idea of the entire year.

"Hey, this is just like the Christmas story!" I shout this because I'm really excited and the bus is loud. "There wasn't room for the real Mary's baby, either! Mrs. Burdon, can we act out the Christmas story on the day of the gift exchange?"

Everyone cheers.

We spend the next week making costumes and wrapping gifts while we plan the play and talk about *Jesus*. I *see* Todd listening, and I'm sure he's planning to make trouble. I put the ball I bought for him in a shoebox and wrap it, and stick it under the tree anyway.

I *see* another box about the same size with my name on it, and I tingle all over. Getting presents is the best.

At lunch recess, Todd stays to talk to Mrs. Burdon. I want to know what he's planning, so I hide outside the door and listen.

"Yes, Jesus loves you, Todd," Mrs. Burdon is saying. "He came to earth as a baby. That's why we celebrate Christmas."

I feel awful. I don't wait to hear the rest. I run to the cafeteria, praying, "Jesus, please forgive me."

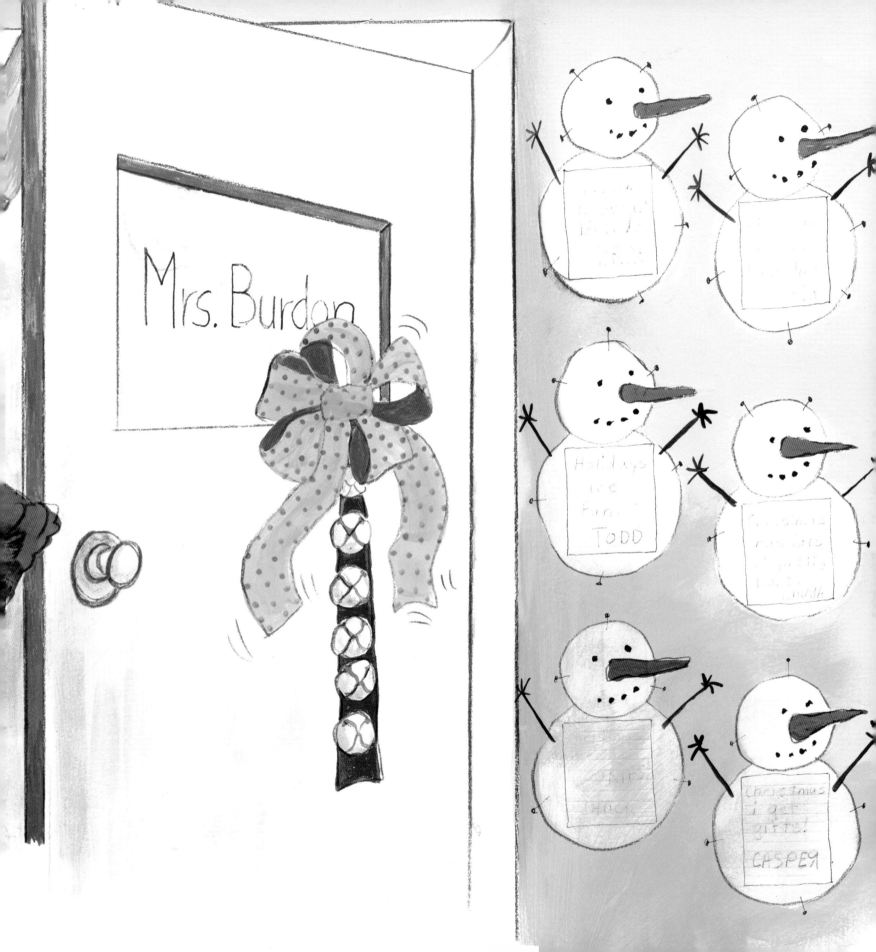

H iI jJ KK Ll Mm

After lunch, I shove
my Wise Man costume toward Todd.
Todd looks puzzled. "Why? Who will you be?"
"I'll be King Herod. Want to help me make a costume?"
"Sure," he says.
Just before the pageant, I unwrap Todd's present, shove the
car into the shoebox, and cram the ball into my pocket.

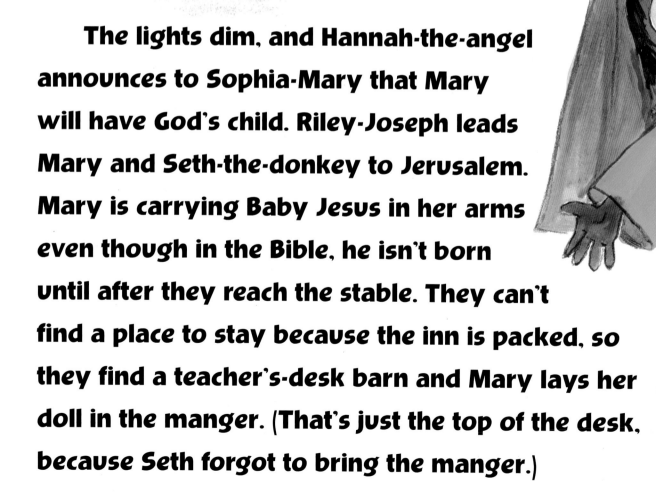

The lights dim, and Hannah-the-angel announces to Sophia-Mary that Mary will have God's child. Riley-Joseph leads Mary and Seth-the-donkey to Jerusalem. Mary is carrying Baby Jesus in her arms even though in the Bible, he isn't born until after they reach the stable. They can't find a place to stay because the inn is packed, so they find a teacher's-desk barn and Mary lays her doll in the manger. (That's just the top of the desk, because Seth forgot to bring the manger.)

Angels announce Jesus' birth to the shepherds, and they all rush in. The Wise Men *see* the star and ask me where they can find Jesus. I cross my arms and *look* mad, because I'm mean ol' King Herod. But I *feel* happy, because Todd's face is shining bright enough to be the star. I can tell he finally understands Jesus is the reason for Christmas. I think he even knows that Jesus loves him.

Afterward, we open presents. When Todd sees the car, his face looks like someone dunked it in joy. My heart feels like it's whirling around in a bucket of happy bubbles. Now I understand that giving presents is even better than getting them.

There's a **HUGE** surprise when I open my present. It's the same awesome car I gave Todd, and a note inside the package says, "First I bought a ball for you at the dollar store. Later, I decided to give you this car. Todd." We grin at each other. I think maybe we'll be friends now.

FOR PARENTS

The Bible forbids judging, yet all through its pages God teaches us how to discern right from wrong. He expects us to observe bad actions and know with a certainty they are wrong. That is being discerning; it is not judging. *Judging means imputing motives to someone when only God knows what is truly in his/her heart.*

Reading it together

As you read, note that all people have flaws and Erik reveals one of his in this book—he sometimes judges people.

Talking it over

How did Erik judge Todd? Discuss how judging another person often results in misjudging them. Let your child talk about a time someone judged him/her. How did it feel? Ask your child if he/she can think of a time when they judged another person.

Taking action

Make a "Jesus Loves Everyone" tree this year. On a glass ball ornament, use a metallic permanent marker to write the name of someone Jesus loves. On the opposite side of the ornament, write one reason Jesus loves him/her. Names of family members and friends will decorate many balls, but the names of enemies should go on some also.

Just for fun

After you finish decorating the tree, switch on the tree lights and pray for the people named on one or two of the ornaments. Do this every evening leading up to Christmas.